BOOK OF
LOVE
POEMS

SARAH A. WASHINGTON

authorHOUSE®

AuthorHouse™
1663 Liberty Drive
Bloomington, IN 47403
www.authorhouse.com
Phone: 1 (800) 839-8640

Published by AuthorHouse 12/28/2017

ISBN: 978-1-5462-2215-6 (sc)
ISBN: 978-1-5462-2214-9 (e)

Contents

FROM THE AUTHOR ESS

I AM KNOWN FOR THE THINGS
I SPEAK THE NAME STAND FOR IT SELF
I ADORE THE SUN SET
I DESIRE A LIFE OF LOVE
I KNOW NO LIMIT TO THE POEMS I CREATE
NORTH / SOUTH/ EAST/ WEST
BUT I AM BOUND IN THE SOUTH
IMPLIED AND SPECIFIED
WITH A POETIC MIND
CREATING A POEM ABOUT
SOMEONE AND THAT SOMEONE
IS YOU

INTRODUCTION

BOOK OF LOVE POEMS
A LITTLE BOOK OF
LOVE POEMS FOUND
FOR EVERYONE
TO BEHOLD IN THEIR ARMS
AND READ:

BELIVETH IT TO RECEIVETH
READ IT TO BELIEVE IT
READ IT AND BELIVETH
BELIEVE IT TO READ IT
POEMS TALKING ABOUT LOVE AND NICE THINGS
LIKE LOVING IN BED
WEDDING BANDS
POETIC THINGS LIKE WALKING IN THE LIGHT OF THE
MOON WITH THE ONE YOU LOVE AND KEEP CLOSE
A STROLL IN THE YARD BEFORE DARK, AND WE WILL BE IN THE PARK
AT DARK IN THE LIGHT OF THE MOON AND
WATCHING THE SUNRISE EARLY IN THE MORNING FROM YOUR
BEDROOM WINDOW
WHILE STILL LOVING IN BED
THING LIKE THAT, THAT ENRICH LOVE AND MARRIAGE

COUNTRY ROAD

STROLLING DOWN THAT OLD COUNTRY ROAD THEIR WAS LOVE TO RECEIVE
EACH MILE YOU STROLL AND AFTER STROLL YOU RECEIVED FAITH
UN AWARE PLACE IN YOUR HEART BY GOD FROM HEAVEN ABOVE
AND LIGHT GIVEN INTO ONE'S MIND TO BRACE THERE SOUL
FOR HEAVEN OPEN UP AND SHADOW PEACE IN THE LAND
AND JOY ON THE EARTH AT THE END OF THE DAY TO MAKE ONE WISE
THE PEOPLE WAS JOYFUL YET THEY KNEW NOT THE KING
BUT GOD BLESS THE STILL AS THEY STROLL FROM DAY TO DAY
DOWN THAT OLD COUNTRY ROAD

THE WICKED

THE WICKED ROSE UP AND STOLE FROM THE STORE
IN THE MIDDLE OF THE NIGHT
GOD SENT DOWN HEAT ON HIS SOUL
AND HE WAS GRIEVED THE HEAT CONSUMED THE WICKNESS
OF HIS MIND
HE BOW AND PRAYED LORD HELP MY SOUL
I HAVE STOLE ROSE AND LIFT HIS HANDS TO HEAVEN
AND PRAISE GOD, THAT I'AM WICKED NO MORE
I HAVE BEEN CHANGED
I'AM A NEW CREATURE IN CHRIST
MY SOUL BEEN DELIVERED FROM HELL
PRAISE, GOD PRAISE GOD
THE GOD OF MY SOUL

GLORY

I LOVE THE NAME OF JESUS
HIS NAME MAKE ONE AWARE OF LOVING HIM AND THE CONSEQUENCE THERE
OF THE EFFECT OF HIS POWER ON ONE SOUL IS JOY
THERE IS GLORY AND POWER FOUND IN HIS NAME AND THE POWER OF HIS
GLORY IS HIS NAME
HIS WORK IS NO GAME BUT GAIN
THERE IS NO SHAME IN IS FAME
THERE IS GLORY AND HONOUR IN HIS NAME
FOR IT FAME TURN TO GLORY BECAUSE OF HIS NAME AND JESUS IS HIS NAME

GOLD

O GOLD
YELLOW GOLD TO
IT MELLOW
IT YELLOW
IT GOLD
FOR HE COMETH WITH GOLD
IN HIS HANDS, AND LOVE
ON HIS MIND AND IN HIS HEART TO
ALL FOR ME MY TYPE OF FELLOW
THOSE ARE THE KIND
I LIKE TO DINE WITH A MAN, DONT MINE BUYING
AND GIVE YOU THE KEY TO HIS HEART TO
AND SAY NOW YOU ARE MINES AND WITH THIS GOLDEN WEDDING BAND
I DO PLAN TO WED-THEE
NOW SAY YES FOR YOU ARE MINES

HAR_MO_NY

LET NOT ONE LOOSE THE HARMONY
OF THEIR HONEYMOON
ONE YEAR AFTER NOON WHEN THE
MOON GOES DOWN DOWN

AND DADDY DONT HAVE A DIME
AND BABY NEED MILK AND START CRYING
WHEN ALL THEIR MONEY IS
GONE AND THE HONEYMOON
IS OVER AND THY CAN NO LONGER LIVE
LIKE A KING AND QUEEN
AND THEIR THRONE COLLAPSE
AND COME TO A RUIN
LOOSE NOT THE HARMONY OF THE
HONEY MOON

Love That Keep

WHEN YOU FIND LOVE
KEEP IT
KEEP IT WARM AND HOT
MAKE SURE IT YOUR OWN LOVE AND NOT SOMEONE ELSE LOVE FOR MUTUAL
LOVE
LOVE THE KEEP YOUR MIND AT EASE BECAUSE I AM IN LOVE WITH SOMEONE
THAT LOVE ME
BE BOLD BE SURE
BE STRONG, KEEP IT WARM AND HOT
DONT LET THE HASSLE OF A DAY
CAUSE YOUR LOVE TO VANISH AWAY
WHEN YOU FIND LOVE
KEEP IT WARM AND KEEP IT HOT
LOVE THAT KEEP

Ir_re_vers_ible

HOW MUCH I LOVE MY HUSBAND
MY LOVE FOR MY HUSBAND IS IRREVERSIBLE
AS HIS LOVE TO ME IS IRREVERSIBLE
I LOVE HIM WITH EVERY BREATH THAT I BREATHE
HE IS LIKE AIR THAT I BREATHE
HE IS PART OF ME INGRAINED IN MY MIND
WE CANNOT BE SEPARETED
WE ARE MARRED AND IN LOVE TO
FOR EVERY THING THAT I DO IS PART OF HIM
FOR HE IS PART OF ME_ FOR WE ARE AS ONE
AND OUR LOVE IS STRONG
WHEN_ AND IF HE DIE BEFORE I DO
I WANT TO GO AND BE NO MORE BECAUSE HE IS PART OF ME
MY LIFE COMPANION
AND OUR LOVE IS IRREVERSIBLE

SHAM_MING

SHAM SHAM SHAMMING
AL I SEE AL AROUND TOWN
MEN PRETENDING TO BE IN LOVE
WHEN THEY ARE ONLY PRETENDING
WHEN THEY WANT SOME_ONE TO ATTEND TO THEIR AFFAIRS
WHILE THEY GO FREE, DASHING DOWN THE STREET
CARE FREE WITH A SMILE ON THEIR FACE, SAYING IN THEIR
HEART
I AM NOT SHAMMING NOW AS IF GOD NOT SEE THEIR HEART
WIFE LEFT AT HOME AL ALONE, WHILE HE GO SHAMMING
AL AROUND TOWN

COLD AS SNOW

IN THE MIDDLE OF WINTER WHEN IT AS COLD AS SNOW
AND THERE IS SNOW, AND THE TABLE IS BARE, NO FOOD
AL IS GONE, AL FACES, SADDEN FOR FEAR OF THE SNOW
STROM COMING
COLD FEET ON THE FLOOR
MA MA NOT HOME
DADDY IS GONE
FOR GRAVEYARD AWAIT OUR SOUL
FOR WE ARE ALONE
NO FOOD OR CLOTHING TO KEEP US WARM
OR OUR SOUL FROM FAMISHING
WE MUST HOLD ON
AND LIVE ON
SPRING WILL SOON COME
AND WE WILL BE ABLE TO TAKE OF OURSELVES
AND THERE WERE A KNOCK ON THE DOOR
I OPEN THE DOOR THERE WERE A NOTE ATTACHED TO
THE DOOR I OPEN THE NOTE THERE WERE A CHECK, AND
A BASKET OF FOOD LARGE ENOUGH FOR THE SPAN OF TIME
WOOD TO KEEP US WARM UNTIL SPING,
I CLOSED THE DOOR AND SHED A TEAR OR TWO
AND THEN WARM OUR FEET AND FEED OUR SOUL
FOR FOR THE SNOW STROM CAME BUT WE DIDN'T
FAMISH NEITHER WERE WE COLD

DARLING

SUN GOES DOWN
SUN COME UP
MY LOVE FOR
YOU DARLING
ALWAYS STAYS UP
THAT THE WAY
MY LOVE IS DARLING
FOR YOU
IT RISE AND SHINE
WITH YOU ON MY MIND

WHITE MOON

WHITE MOON
I LOVE TO VIEW
HIGH IN THE SKY
SEATED ON MAJESTIC BLUE AT NOON
WHITE MOON, STAND STRONG FIRM AND TALL
FIX IN THE SKY AND UNMIX
FOR ALL TO VIEW
HIGH IN THE SKY
A AMAZING VIEW TO
SEE WHITE MOON, MOON AT NOON

EVERLASTING RED ROSES

RED ROSES
     MY SPOUSE SENT
                  MY SPOUSE SENT ME ONE DOZENS
        TO SHOW HIS LOVE ON VALENTINE DAY
      HIS EVERLASTING LOVE AS A RED ROSE
     FOR ME TO CHERISH DAY TO DAY
    UNDER THE EVENING STAR
EVERLASTING RED ROSES   TO SHOW HIS LOVE

SEALED IN A VASE OF CRYSTAL LEAD
WITH GOLD

           SIGNED IN LETTER OF PURE
GOLD:
    I LOVE YOU
       FOREVER

SEVEN

THE CHURCH HAD A PREACHING MEETING
LAST NIGHT, THEY TRIED TO PREACH THE TOWN
DOWN.
EVERYONE IN TOWN, CAME AROUND WHEN THEY
HEARD THE SOUND
THE SINGERS SONG, SUNGS TO GOD AND THE CHURCH _ REJOICED AND
REJOICED
THE BACKSLIDERS CAME BACK AND LIFTED UP THEIR HANDS TO
GOD AND SAID I GOT A RIGHT
TO PRAISE GOD TO LORD TAKE AWAY MY SINS
THE NIGHT CLUB CLOSED THEIR DOORS
EVERYONE FELL DOWN ON THE FLOOR TO THEIR KNEES
AND START PRAYING WHEN THEY KNEW THEIR NAME WERE
BLOTTED OUT OF THE BOOK OF LIFE IN HEAVEN
AND ROLL INTO THE HOUSE OF GOD
PLEADING AND BEGGING FOR FORGIVEN OF THEIR SIN
AND THERE WERE NO END TO THE MEN THAT CAME IN
THE LADIES AND CHILDREN RAN BEFORE THE MEN IN A WHIRLWIN AND
ENTERED IN
SAYING LORD, O GOD WHERE IS MY NAME IN THE BOOK OF
ETERNAL LIFE SAYING I GOT A RIGHT TO PRAISE

G
 O
  D _TO

My Pa

MY PA
MY PA, WAS A SHARE CROPPER
HE WORK FROM DAY'S DAWN TO THE GOING DOWN OF THE EVENING
SUN ON THE FARM,
HE FEED HIS FAMILY OF 10 ON 2 HEN AND TEN DOLLARS
PER WEEK AND SOMETIME LESS THAN THAT
HE LABORED OF AND ON EVEN OUT OF HIS SLEEP
HE CHOPPED DOWN TREES FROM THE WOOD TO KEEP HIS FAMILY WARM
AND FOR COOKING PURPOSE TO
MA SENT THE DOG AWAY FOR THERE WAS NOT ENOUGH FOOD TO FEED
THE DOG TO.
AND THEN ONE COLD DREARY WINTER DAY AT DUSK PA WENT TO
GATHER WOOD FOR THE STOVE TO KEEP HIS FAMILY WARM
HE SLEW A TREE AND THE TREE SLEW HIM
HE DIED AND SO DID THE TREE
I WAS OVERWELL BY THE GRIEF NO ONE FELT
WHEN RETURN HOME AFTER MY PA_ WAS DEAD AND GONE
AND STILL FEEL IT IN MY SOUL EACH NIGHT WHEN I PRAY
THOSE OLD STOVES I KEEP AND CHERISH IN MY HOME
EVEN UNTO THIS DAY
MY PA THE SHARE CROPPER DEAD AND GONE MANY
LONG YEARS AGO

SUGAR CUBES

THE WORDS OF MY MOUTH
ARE LIKE SUGAR CUBES
HAST CAME OUT OF MY HEART
INTO MY MIND AND THEY TASTE SWEET TO
THEY ARE READY TO GO OUT
AND START SOMETHING
SOMETHING GREAT
LIKE FINDING THAT MAN LOST IN THE WILDNESS
WITHOUT A WEDDING BAND
WITH A TREASURE IN HIS FIELD OF WHITE GOLD
AND A HOME THAT STAND AS A CASTLE WITHOUT A QUEEN
WAITING FOR A QUEEN TO KISS HIS LIPS
TO RECEIVE THE SUGAR HE HAST BEEN, LONGING
FOR AND TO PLACE THAT WEDDING BAND OF PURE GOLD ON HER
FINGER

EVER_MORE

EVERMORE I WILL BE LOVING YOU
EVEN MORE
KISSES OF LOVE I SEND YOU IN THE SKY
TO WALK OVER YOUR HEAD
WHERE EVER YOU GO
YOUR PAIN AND SORROW
I CRUSH TO JOY IN AND HOUR
BECAUSE I LOVE YOU_ SO
EVEN MORE

COURAGE

THE WORDS OF THY MOUTH
ARE LIKE A BUNDLE OF JOY
THEY TAKE AWAY SADDNESS
AND GIVE GLADNESS
AND INSPIRE
LOVE AND COURAGE
GIVE WISDOM
AND MAKE ONE WISE
THE WORDS OF THY
MOUTH IS WHAT
I HEARD THAT
GAVE ME COURAGE

****** STARRING NIGHT ******

STARRED NIGHT, A SIGHT TO SEE
IN THE SKY, A BEAUTIFUL SIGHT
THAT WILL NOT FADE AWAY IN
MEMORY
THE MOON LIGHT EVER SO BRIGHT AND BEAUTIFUL
GOLDEN YELLOW IN COLOR
A TREASURE OF MEMORY IN ONE NIGHT
A SIGHT TO SEE IN THE SKY
HIGH ABOVE IN THE HEAVEN
STARRING NIGHT

SORROW

IT WILL TAKE SORROW AND NOT JOY
TO KEEP HIM HERE UNTIL TOMORROW
HIS MIND IS WANDERING IN THE LAND
HIS JOY IS GONE HE HAST LOST
HIS LOVE FOR WHOM HE DID WED
SIN HAST CAPTURE HIS MIND
HATE HAST CAME IN
IT WILL TAKE GOD __TO BRING BACK HIS LOVE
AND GIVE HIM JOY
LET HIM BE GONE TODAY
GOD WILL BRING HIM BACK TOMORROW
WHEN HE HAS WASH AWAY HIS SORROW
AND HIM BACK LOVE AND JOY

LOVE CONQUERS

LOVE CONQUERS ALL THINGS.
YOU CONQUER MY HEART
YOU FILL MY EYES WITH
THE SIGHT OF YOU
YOU GAVE ME YOUR LOVE
WHEN YOU DIDN'T KNOW ME
YOU HOLD MY VIEW OF THE
LOVE OF YOU
I CAN FELL OUR LOVE _AGREE
IN HEART
AND WE WILL NEVER SAY BY AND BY
AND FAR WELL TO ONE ANOTHER
OUR LOVE HAS CONQUER OUR HEART
FOR LOVE CONQUERS ALL THINGS
AND LOVE HAS CONQUEROUR HEART

P<small>OEM</small> F<small>OR</small> T<small>HE</small> C<small>HURCH</small>

EXCEPT NO SIN WHEN YOU STAND FOR CHRIST
FOR IT NOT RIGHT
FOR A MAN TO DIVOCE HIS WIFE
TO MARRIAGE HIS SISTER IN CHRIST
AVOID IT, BE NOT A PART OF IT
IT A GREAT DELUSION
STRENGTHEN NOT YOURSELVES IN SIN
AND LOOSE YOUR SOUL IN THE END
FOR SATAN WILL WEAKEN YOU_DOWN
AND BY THIS TIME TO_MORROW YOU WILL BE
READY TO DIVOCE HER IN ORDER TO
MARRY ANOTHER

GOD LOVE

GOD LOVE IS TRUE
LOVE LOVE IS PURE
GOD LOVE LOVE IS HERE
GOD LOVE IS OVER THERE
GOD LOVE IS FAR
GOD LOVE IS NEAR
GOD LOVE IS AROUND US
GOD LOVE SURROUNDS US
FOR IT'S ALL AROUND US
EVEN WITHIN US
CAN HIS BE FOUND

SPRING LOVE******
****** SPRING TIME LOVE

SPRING LOVE
IS IN THE AIR
SEE HOW EVERYTHING
IS GROWING
LIFE ENRICHED BY THE
AIR WE BREATHE
AND THE THINGS WE SEE
AND THE THINGS WE DO
GREEN GRASS EVERWHERE AND TREES
AND THE WORDS WE HEAR AND SPEAK
AND THE PEOPLE WE MEET
AND THE FRIENDS WE MAKE
WE ARE ENPOWER WITH
THE SPRING OF LOVE
FROM HEAVEN ABOVE
GLORY BE TO GOD

F
 O
  R   T
          H   LOVE
           E   OF   L
                            O
                             V
                              E,

WISDOM

WHAT SISTER MARY.
SAID TO BROTHER BERRY
THAT APPROACH HER
THAT WAS NOT WISE
YOU ARE TO HEAD STRONG FOR ME
I READ MY BIBLE
I BELIVE WHAT I READ
AND I KNOW WHAT
I BE HOLD
I DONT SEE ME LOVING YOU
ARE WANTING YOU
SO DONT TRY TO PERSUADE IN VAIN
SO IF YOU EXCUSE I WILL CONTINUE
TO READ MY BIBLE AND TALK TO GOD
UNDER THE BLUE SKY
AND BE FREE FROM YOU
THE WISDOM OF GOD HAS REVEALED AND SEAL
IT TO FOR WISDOM CAN BE FOUND IN GOD SO BE WISE

A
L
E
T
T
E
R

                    HI TOM
ALL THE LETTERS OF TRASH
I RECEIVE I PLACE
THEM IN FILE 1 3
YOU CAN PLACE
YOUR LETTER
OVER_ THERE TO

MARCH ON

BE NOT OFF
FROM YOUR
PRAYER TO GOD
BY ODYESEY
KEEP YOUR EYES ON GOD
AND MARCH ON
OFFEND NO_ ONE
MARCH ON
YOU ARE A SOLDIER
OF GOD NOW
MARCH ON

CROSS_WORD LOVE

CROSSWORD LOVE IS LIKE A PUZZLE
SOME MEN LOVE IS LIKE A CROSSWORD
PUZZLE YOU NEED CLUES
TO LOVE THEM
FIND THE CLUE TO DIMISS THEM

CROSSWORD LOVE DIMISS

BRAVO

BE NOT IMPRESS
WHEN THE CROWD
SHOUT, BRAVO, BRAVO
AND NO ONE STAND FOR THE DEFENCE OF THE CAUSE
FOR THERE ARE NINE SINS
CONCEALED WITHIN
THEY WILL CHEER YOU ON
JUST TO KEEP THEM FROM BEING REVEALED

AUTOGRAPH LOVE

AUTOGRAPH LOVE, SIGN IN MY BED
I WILL NEVER SLEEP WITH ANOTHER
DARLING FOR I CAN'T GET OVER YOU
YOU AUTOGRAPH MY HEART
YOU ARE STILL IN MY HEART
ERODING MY MIND FOR A TOUCH OF YOUR
LOVE
MY SOUL IS FREE
BUT I CONTINUE TO
THINK OF YOU NIGHT AND DAY
THE TIME WE SPENT TOGETHER
AUTOGRAPH

                                  LOVE

GET OVER YOU   I WILL NEVER

CANDLE LIGHT DINNER

DINNER WILL BE SERVED LATE
DARLING I LOVE TO DINE IN CANDLE LIGHT
LATE AT NIGHT
IN THE LIGHT OF THE MOON

AND LET THE SHADOW OF THE MOON
SHINE DOWN ON YOU
AND ABSORB YOUR MASCULINE CHARM
AND LOVE TO
IN THE CANDLE LIGHT

POEM******
*****
****

POEM OF MY LOVE
TRUE TO MY SOUL
GRACE FOR MY LIPS
BOLD TO BE SPOKEN
TRUE TO BELIEVE
NICE TO BE_ HOLD
CAN'_T BE DREAMED
ONLY BELIEVED
POEM OF MY LOVE

MY BUDGET

LET YOUR BUDGET BE LIKE YOUR PAY CHECK
PLAIN AND SIMPLE
FIRM AND STRONG
FIX AND STREAM_ LINE
LIKE YOUR PAY CHECK
LIVE WITH_ IN YOUR BUDGET
LET YOUR BUDGET REFLECT YOUR CHECK
MY BUDGET

CHERRY LIPS

CHERRY LIPS
DID YOU FEEL THEM FLOATING IN THE AIR
GOING HOME TO YOU
IN WORDS OF COLOR OF CHERRY
JUST FOR YOU CHERRY LIPS
COMING HOME TO YOU
I SEND THE LOVE OF MY LIPS
AND I WILL BE THERE SOON
CHERRY LIPS COMING HOME   TO
                              Y
                               O
                                U

Prompt

MY PEN IS PROMPT
NO PUT ON
READY TO TACKLE THE ACTION
READY TO WRITE THE FACTS
AND FAX THE FACTS
AND TELL THE NEWS
OF THE COUNTRY BLUES
CONCERT IN TOWN THE MALE VOCALIST
STARTED TO SING I WILL BE LOVING YOU SOON
LADIES BEGIN
                 TO FAINT
I STEP ASIDE
AND SAID I AM ONLY HERE TO TAKE THE NEWS AND RECORDS
THE FACTS_____ AND MY PEN IS PROMPT
AND WILL NOT MIS PRINT

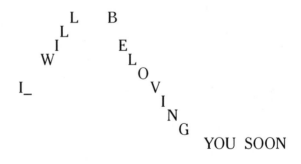

BE_FALL
BEHOLD

I WILL NOT BEFALL NOR BEHOLD
LOVE

LOVE CAN BE LIKE RAIN DROPS LOVE YOU AND LEAVE YOU
LOVE CAN BE AS SNOW IN THE WINTER AS COLD AS SNOW
LOVE CAN BE AS THE AUTUM FROST, ON THE LAND
WHEN THE SUN COME UP IT GOES AWAY
LOVE CAN BE AS A SPRING DAY THAT DONT LAST

LOVE CAN BE AS HOT AS A SUMMER DAY

AND VANISH AWAY TO
THAT WHY I NOT LET LOVE BE_FALL ME NOR BE_HOLD ME
LOVE CAN BE LIKE A ROLL_ER COASTER

I WILL NOT BE_HOLD IT

SWEET

THE MAN CHARM IS, SWEET, SWEET, SWEET
HE SWEEP ME OF MY FEET
AND CONTINUE TO GET SWEETER
I WANT TO GET CLOSER
FOR I KNOW THAT YOU ARE FOR REAL
AND I AM LONGING TO BE
EMBRACE IN YOUR ARMS
AND I AM IMPRESS BY_ YOUR CHARM

DAWN

SOME TIME I TYPE FROM DUSK TO DAWN
AND NAKED TO
NO TIME TO PUT CLOTHES ON AFTER
I SHOWER
MY PEN_ AWAIT_ MY TOUCH
READY TO WORK
WE FIGHT THE FIGHT TO WRITE ALL
NIGHT LONE UNTIL _DAWN AND I WIN

    MY COFFEE STAYS _HOT
    MY PEN READY TO WRITE
    AND I AM NAKED TO

    SO DONT HOLD ME BACK LET ME GO

RAG_GED

FOR MY CLOTHING AS A CHILD WAS
FROM RAG TO RAG
WITHOUT A TAG
IN A BROWN BAG
A BAG OF RAGGED RAGS
PASS DOWN
AND SET ON THE GROUND
FOR THE POOR OF THE LAND
THAT WAS FROWN ON
RAGGED RAGS DID I WEAR ALL AROUND
TOWN

MY DAUGHTER

I WANT TO THANK YOU
FOR BEING MY DAUGHTER
MY LITTLE GIRL THAT
GROWN_UP
INTO A WOMAN
AND NOW I MUST LET YOU KNOW
THAT MARRIAGE SOME_TIME FAIL
AND LOVE DONT ALL WAYS LAST
SO BE GROWN AS A WOMAN AND
WALK_ AWAY
FROM THAT WHICH HAS FAILED
MY DAUGHTER

OVER IN JUNE

I AM STILL A POET___AND POETIC
I SIT AT MY DESK
TO WRITE LOVELY THINGS
I SEE AND FELL IN MY MIND AND HEART
AND THANK GOD THAT I AM NOT GRIEVED
BUT JOYFUL
FOR I HEARD IN THE WIND THAT LOVE
WAS COMING IN JUNE
NO IT SOONER THAN THAT
IT WILL BE OVER IN JUNE

FAME

FAME AND RICHES ON EARTH
IS GREAT FOR WE ALL WOULD
LOVE TO CHERISH THE FAME
BUT ONLY THE RICH RECEIVE
BUT HELL IS WORSE THAN FAME
AND WE ALL ARE GONE TO FEEL THE
PAIN OF HEEL IF DONT PRAISE HIM
SO LET US ALL CHERISH LOVE
AND SEEK ETERNAL LIFE
ABOVE THAT FAME
    AND REJOICE BECAUSE OUR NAME
    IS WTITTEN IN HEAVEN
          IN THE BOOK OF ETERNAL LIFE
        AND NOT BE BLOTTED _ OUT

WONDERFUL THINGS

I ONLY DO WONDERFUL THINGS
LIKE LOVING YOU 24 HOURS AROND THE CLOCK
AND SENDING YOU MY LOVE IN THE AIR
AND WONDERING WHAT YOU ARE DOING WHEN YOU ARE
NOT HOME WITH ME
AND DREAMING OF YOU WHEN I SLEEP
AND BAKING A PIE FOR YOU AND FILL IT WITH MY
LOVE TO EAT
THOSE ARE THE WONDERFUL THINGS I DO BECAUSE I AM IN LOVE WITH
YOU

DONT

DONT START MY IMAGINATION OF POWER
ON YOU TO THINK
FOR THERE IS NO END_ TO THE THINGS I MIGHT
THINK OF YOU

AND NO TELLING WHAT I MIGHT WRITE OF YOU
FOR I AM POET
I TRY TO BE WISE AND NOT SAD
      BECAUSE I CAN NOT ALL WAYS WRIT WHAT I
DONT SEE

BOWLING

FOR HE IS A MAN WITH SKILL AND CHARM
A BOLD PROFESSIONAL
I WOULD LIKE TO BE PART OF HIS TEAM AND
BOWEL WITH HIM TO HELP HIM_ ACCOMPLISH HIS
PLAN AND MY PLAN TO BY BOWELING WITH HIM
WANTING TO BOWEL WITH HIM

THY LOVETH

THY LOVETH HER NOT
THY LOVETH HER NOT BECAUSE SHE IS NOT THY
WIFE
THY LOVETH HER NOT BECAUSE THY WANT HER TO BE
THY WIFE AND SHE BE_LONGETH TO ANOTHER
AND THY LOVETH HER NOT
BUT SEEKETH ANOTHER TO BE THY WIFE

STAY WITH THEE

SHALL NOT I SEETH THEE TO_MORROW
VERILY TRUELY I WANT TO STAY WITH THEE
THY LOVE IS LOVE TO ME A LOVE I NEVER
FELT BEFORE
I NEEDETH NO WINE TO MAKE MY HEART MERRY
I FEELETH MERRY BY BEING WITH THEE
I NEED NO STRONG TO GIVE ME COURAGE TO LOVE THEE
THY LOVE OVER SHADOW ME
I SHALL STAY WITH THEE

LOVE

BRING ME YOUR LOVE LIKE A DOVE
AND DROP IT ON ME
I WILL BE WAITING FOR YOU MY LOVE
IN YOUR BED WITH LOVE
I WILL PICK UP AND WILL BE WAITING
ON YOU
       WITH LOVE

A MAN
SEEKING

THY STANDETH STRONG LIKE A TOWER
HIGH DO THY STAND AS A STRONG TOWER
IN THY VOICE I DETECT THY SEEKETH LOVE_
TO WIFE THY LOOKETH FOR THE FAIREST
AMONG THE WOMEN OF THE LAND TO WED
TO BE THY WIFE
MANY WATERS
     WILL NOT BE ABLE TO QUENCH
THY LOVE FOR HER WHEN THY FINDETH HER
A MAN SEEK ING A WIFE

THEY KNOW

A POEM OF POETRY NO ONE WANT TO HEAR
BECAUSE THEY KNOW IT ABOUT THEM
SO THEE DONT WANT TO FACE THE TRUTH
THEN THEY SAYLET US HEAR ABOUT
SOMEONE ELSE NOT ME I WILL HEAR
LATER I AM BUSY THIS DAY
THEY ARE AFRAID TO FACE THE FACTS
THE POEM OF POERTY NO ONE TO HEAR CONTAINS FACTS
ABOUT THEM
NOT MONEY OR FAME
FRIEND OR LOVE
THINGS LIKE THAT IT'S
ALL ABOUT THEM

READY TO BE

LET OUR LOVE FLOURISH AS THE GREEN _ GRASS
WHEN IT COMETH FORTH FROM THE EARTH
I AM READY TO BE MARRIED TO YOU MY
BE_LOVE
MAKE HASTE MY BE_LOVE
OUR WEDDING NIGHT IS HERE
LETETH THY HAND BE READY TO PLACE THY WEDDING BAND ON MY FINGER

MY LIPS ARE WARM FOR THY LOVE AND HOT KISSES IN OUR BED MY
BELOVE READY TO BE THY WIFE

OVER YOUNDER

POEM COMING FROM OVER YOUNDER
NOT A DISTANCE
WAITING TO BE RECEIVED
BOUND TO AWAKEN
YOUR MIND AND GIVE YOU A POUNDING HEART
TO BELIEVE
WANTING TO BE RECORDED ALL ABOUT YOU TO
FROM OVER YOUNDER

MOVING AGAIN

HOLD IT DOWN ALL THE WAY TO THE GROUND
MOVE NO MORE TRY TO AVOID
LOOSE THOSE POUND SAVE THE CASH
REAP THE PRIZE OF NOT MOVING
AGAIN__ HOLDING THE CASH DOWN TO THE
GROUND

My Words

MY WORDS HAS STARTED AND THEY WILL NOT END UNTIL
I AM COMPLED SPEAKING IN A POEM OF LIFE
OF THE LOVE I LOST
AND NOW UPHOLD THE RIGHT NOT TO LOVE
AGAIN
_____ MY WORDS

/ WHENCE

WHENCE KNOWEST
THY MY LOVE
I AWAIT FOR THEE
UNDER THE BIG OAK TREE
THY PASSETH ME BY LIKE A BIRD IN THE SKY
LIKE A DOVE THY PASSETH ME BY
KNOWEST NOT THAT I WERE THERE
AND WAIT FOR THY LOVE
UNDER THE OAK TREE
SEETH ME NOT MY LOVE
DOWN UNDER THE OLD OAK TREE
SETTING UNDER THE TREE WAITING FOR THEE
WHENCE COMETH NOT MY LOVE TO BE WITH ME.

MY BELOVE

MY BELOVE
THY LOVE MY LOVE
HAST BEND A SHIELD
FOR ME IT KEEPETH ME WARM FROM THE COLD
THY LOVE INCREASETH MY LOVE FOR THEE
IT MAKETH ME SMILE
WHEN I SEE THEE
AND GLAD WHEN THY TOUCHETH ME
I SPEAK THE TRUTH I SPEAK LOVE IN WORD
FROM WITHIN MY SOUL HOW I LOVETH
THEE MY BELOVE

JOY_FUL VOICE

THY VOICE WAS JOYFUL
WHEN I HEARD THEE SINGING A SONG
ABOUT ME IN THE DARK OF THE NIGHT IN THE
TWILIGHT OF THE STARRY NIGHT
ABOUT THE LADY NEXT DOOR
THAT I DESIRE TO DINE WITH AND SHARE A GLASS OF
WINE
FOR I CAN NOT STAND THE THOUGHT OF
LOOSING HER TO ANOTHER
I AM NOT GOING TO LOOSE HER TO ANOTHER
I AM GOING TO KNOCK ON THAT DOOR AND SING
HER THIS SONG

AROUND/ BED

WHEN ROSES ARE ALL AROUND YOUR BED
EVEN AT THE FOOT OF YOUR BED
LIKE A SHOTGUN OVER YOUR HEAD
BE NOT _DISCOURAGED OR DISMAYED
ROSES ARE THERE TO KEEP YOUR SOUL ALIVE
SATAN HOPE YOU DEAD
TO SIN FOR HIM
ROSES AROUND YOUR BED KEEPETH YOUR
SOUL ALIVE

UNTIL

BE NOT GRIEVED WHEN I SPEAK
NOR BE GLAD WHEN
I SPEAKETH NOT
BUT WAIT UNTIL
I SPEAK
BE GLAD OF WHAT THOU HEARETH
ANOTHER SPEAK WAIT UNTIL
I SPEAK

ANOTHER

I WILL NOT LET SORROW
DIM MY LOVE AND HOLD ME BACK THY HAST TAKEN
THY WEDDING RING OF AND NOW THY GIVETH
THY LOVE TO ANOTHER
THY HAST CAST MY LOVE ASIDE
I AM TRODDEN DOWN CAST ASIDE
AND FORGOTTEN
BECAUSE THY ARE IN LOVE WITH ANOTHER

DREAD
OF THE NIGHT

I FIND PLEASURE IN YOUR LOVE_ALWAYS
MY BELOVED
DOUBT NOT MY LOVE
WHEN I RETURN HOME AND I AM BURDEN DOWN
FROM THE TASKS OF THE DAY AND THE DREAD OF
THE NIGHT OF LABORING UNTIL MIDNIGHT AND
UNTIL ALL TASKS DONE AND DONE WELL
AND THAT INCLUDE LOVING YOU UNTIL YOU
SAY ENOUGH LOVE MY LOVE FOR TONIGHT++
LOVE IS FINE IT DONT COST A DIME, BUT LOVE CAN'T
PAY THE BILLS WE NEED THE DIME TO HELP
PAY THE BILLS
I WILL CONTINUE TO LABOR AND LOVE YOU TO UNTIL
WE GET MORE THAN A DIME THEN I WILL LET YOU LABOR
ALONE AND CONTINUE TO LOVE YOU, I FIND PLEASURE IN
YOUR LOVE

ELOPE

MY EYES HAST SEEN THY LOVE AND THY FACE FOR ME AND MY
HEART SHOUT FOR JOY!
THY IS IN LOVE WITH ME LET US ELOPE TOGETHER
SOON AND GET MARRIED AT MIDNIGHT

My Beloved

YOUR LOVE IS LIKE THE SUMMER DEW
IT RE_FRESH MY HEART
I AM GLAD TO BE IN LOVE WITH YOU
YOUR LOVE DE_LIGHT MY HEART
BECAUSE YOU ARE MY BE_LOVE
MY BELOVED SPOUSE
THOU SAIDTH UNTO ME THOU ARE LIKE THE
SUMMER DEWI WILL STAY IN LOVE WITH YOU
MY BE_LOVED SPOUSE

STRONG WORDS

MY FELLOW LOVE FOR ME IS LIKE THE
NOTH WIND IT WILL BLOW DOWN EVERY_ONE
THAT TRYS TO BLOCK HIM FROM ME
HIS WORDS IS STRONG AND STROMY
HE WILL SEND THEM AWAY FLYING IN THE STROM

SUN_LIGHT OF THE DAY

HENCE COMETH THY MY BELOVED
MY DEAR BELOVE THAT I HOPE TO BE MY
SPOUSE WALKETH IN THE SUNLIGHT
OF THE DAY SHINNING DOWN UPON THEE
MIGHTY WEIGHT DOETH THY CARRY ON THY
SHOULDERS TO ASK MY PA PA TO WEDME IN THE
MIDDLE OF DAY KNOWING THAT I DOES LOVE THEE
AND THAT I AM HIS ONLY DAUGHTER AND DEARLY
LOVED
FEAREST THY NOT FROM THE HEAT OF HIS WORDS
AND SWIFT LOOK
IN THE SUN_LIGHT OF THE DAY

64

COMING

WORDS ARE COMING FORTH OUT OF MY HEART
MY MIND CAN NOT SUSTAIN IT
BUT MY PEN CAN WRITE IT
THEY ARE POURING DOWN ON ME OVER
FLOWING MY HEART
THE WORDS OF THIS POEM COMING FORTH OUT
OF MY MIND
TELLING ME WHAT I OUGHTEST TO WRITE
MY MIND CAN NOT BE_LIVE IT
BUT MY PEN CAN WRITE IT

Nu_grape

I NEED NO GIN_SENG WINE OR BRAN_DY TO TAKE
AWAY MY FEAR
NUGRAPE IS WHAT I WANT TO GIVE ME CHEER
IN THE DARKNESS OF THE NIGHT WHEN THE SOUND
OF FEAR IS NEAR AND THE ONLY SOUND THEY HEAR
IS THE SOUND OF FEAR
AND ONE CAN NOT SEE BEFORE THEIR FACE
BRAVERLY STEP FOWARD AND CAPTURE THE DARKNESS
AND SLAYED FEARBLACK NIGHT
RAN AWAY UNTO THE MOON AND THE
LIGHT OF THE MOON CAME FORTH AND WE WALK ON
ACROSS THE RAILROAD TRACK TO THE STORE
THERE I RECEIVED MY NUGRAPE DRINK TO TAKE
AWAY MY FEAR OF FEAR
NOW I RECEIVE MY NU_GRAPE DRINK TO GIVE ME
CHEER

SLEEPING ON THE FLOOR

SLEEPING ON THE FLOOR
LYING ON THE FLOOR
SLEEPING BELOW THE STOVE IN THE COLD OF THE
WINTER TO KEEP WARM _ NO BED TO SLEEP IN
PROUD TO BE BORN
AND A GIRL TO/ NO PRETTY CLOTHES OR BED OF
MY OWEN YET I WAS BORN AND BORN TO THE
POOR
A NIGHT TO REMEMBER AS I GROW OLD
SLEEPING ON THE FLOOR BE_LOW THE
STOVE _____ IN THE COLD

THE JELLY CAKE

RUBY CAKE THE JELLY CAKE
THE SWEETEST CAKE I EVER ATE
I DO REMEMBER SISTER JELLY CAKE
A HOME MADE CAKE
THAT SAVED THE DAY
OF TRAVEL A CAKE BAKED FOR TRAVEL
KEPT EVERYONE HAPPY AS WE ROAD ALONE THE
WAY IN EXPECTION OF THE SWEETEST CAKEVERE
MADE RUBY JELLY CAKE

SAME TIME

IN THAT OLD COUNTRY LAND ON THE FARM
AT THE SAME TIME
IN THE LAND APPLES SOLD FOR A NICKLE OR DIME
RED GREEN AND SOME YELLOW
IF A FELLOW CAME NEAR YOUR FEET YOU KNEW HE
BELONG TO YOU
HE WOULD ASK FOR A DATE AND PICK YOU UP AT NINE
OFF TO SUNDAY AND NOT LATE
EVERY SUNDAY AT THE SAME TIME

ALL_AROUND COLD

LYING IN THE BED IN THE COLD
LYING IN THE COLD IT WAS HARD
NOT TO TAKE A HOLD ON COLD
AND KEEP IN YOUR SOUL
EVEN THE AIR THAT ONE BREATH WAS COLD
COLD WOULD KEEP YOU IN BED ALL NIGHT
LONG UNTIL EARLY MORNING WHEN
THE FLAME OF FIRE WOULD COME_IN
AND A_WAKEN YOUR SOUL
FROM THE COLD

ANCIENT TIME

IN THE ANCIENT DAYS IN THE COUNTRY
WATER WAS TO HOT TO DRINK IN THE SUMMER
TO COLD TO DRINK IN THE WINTER
NOT ENOUGH IN SPRING TO DRINK
DISTANCE WAS MUCH TO FAR TO TRAVEL TO
RECEIVE
IN ANCIENT TIME THE DAYS OF OLD TIME

PRE'CIOUS SOUL

IF THY LIVEST IN SIN
AND SEND FORTH THY LOVE IN HATRED
THY SOUL ARE BOUND TO RECEIVE THE
RE'WARD OF DEATH
DEATH OF THY SOUL WILL BE GRANTED TO
TO THY SOUL
THY SOUL IS PRECIOUS LET NOT
THE STAIN OF DEATH OF DEATH KEEP THY
SOUL

DE'LIGHTED

MY SOUL DELIGHT IN JOY OF WORK_ING WILLFUL
TO PROVIDE FOR THE THING I NEED TO GIVE JOY
OF THE RE_WARD OF MY WORK_ING LABOR DAILY
I AM GLAD TO BE ABLE TO LABOR IN THE LAND
I AM DE'LIGHTED IN THE JOY OF WORKING

LOVE

I SOUGHT LOVE
BUT I FOUND IT NOT
I WAITED FOR MY BELOVED
BUT HE CAME_NOT
I SOUGHT JOY BUT
IT WENT A'WAY
I ASKED FOR HELP BUT I RE'CEIVED IT NOT
SATAN CAME FORTH
BUT I CAST HIM AWAY
I STOOD STILL AND RECEIVED GOD GRACE
I FOUND A LOVE THAT KEEP ME SAFE

VISION

I RECEIVED A DAY VISION OF THEE DECLINING A STAIR CASE
ALL DRESSED IN A WHITE WEDDING GOWN PURE AS
WHITE GOLD/THY BELOVED ARRIVE
ON AN ARROW THROWN BY THE KING
DRESSED IN A ARMOR OF YELLOW GOLD
CARRING THY LUDDAGE WITHOUT A WEDDING BAND
HE TOOK THEE BY_ THE ARM AND LIFTED UP
THY HAND THEE RECEIVED THY WEDDING BAND
IN THE SKY FROM THY BELOVED
THEE LEFT OFF FLYING IN THE AIR TO PARIS
ON THEIR WEDDING NIGHT

THY SERVETH
THY SERVETH

THY SERVETN ME PRECIOUS FRUIT IN MY BED
THY FEEDEST AND LOVETH ME AS WELL/ THY
CHERISH ME AND GIVETH ALL THY LOVE EACH
AND AND EVERY DAY THE SAME TO ME NOW
I CANN'T GET OVER YOU MY BE_LOVE
THAT SERVETH ME
KNOWTH THY I WILL BE HOME AND LOVING THE
THOUGHTS OF THEE WHILE THOU ARE A'WAY
FROM ME

TOWARD

WHEN I LOOK TO WARD THE WILD'NESS
I REMEMBER MY SPOUSE THAT LEFT ME BOUNDED
IN THE WILDNESS AND WENT INTO TOWN
AND MARRIED ANOTHER AND GAVE HIS KEYS
AND SCARF TO ANOTHER AND LEFT ME BOUND
DOWN IN THE WILDNESS
DESTROYED MY LOVE AND HIS LOVE TO HER
HE GAVE HIS NEW LOVE

Be Aware Ladies

HOT PAIN, COLD PAIN, GROWING PAIN, DULL PAIN/
SHARP PAIN, LABOR PAIN/ PAIN LIKE A FLAME
BABY BEING BORN
HUSBAND NOT HOME CALL FROM THE
TELEPHONE IN THE VALLY BUYING HIS BELOVE
A WEDDING BAND
PLAN TO ELOPE TONIGHT
AND MARRY IN THE MOONLIGHT
WHILE THE BABY BEING BORN
ON HIS UNCLE FARM THERE THEY WILL LIVE
UNTIL BABY COME HOME

COMING HOME

I HAVE BEING WEEPING AND CRYING ALL NIGHT
FOR MY BE LOVE TO COME HOME TO ME
FOR HE MUST BE FAR
FOR HE IS NOT HOME
I HAVE BEING AWAING FOR MY LOVE STARING ING THE
SKY LIGHT WAITING FOR HIM TO COME TO ME
ALL NIGHT LONG
AND HE COMETH NOT
FOR HE IS GONE AND NOT COMING BACK
I WILL CRY NO MORE MY LOVE IS NOT COMING/ BACK

RUN_NING

THOU RUNNING DOWN THE ROAD
AS IF IT WERE FOR THE FEAR OF THY SOUL
THOU HEARD THE VOICE WHAT IT SAID AND
WHAT WAS TOLD_ RUN ON AND DONT WALK FOR THE TRAIN IS WAITING
AT THE END OF THE ROAD
OWN ITS WAY HOME YOUR HOME
AND OUR HOME

DEAD/LINE

I GOT A DEAD_ LINE TO KEEP
IT ENDS AT SIX
I GOT TO BE THERE BY SIX
NO SKIPPING ARE HOPING
PER'MIT'TED ON THE WAY
TO GET THERE NO TIME TO READ THE
HEADLINE FOR I AM THE
HEADLINE AND NEED TO BE THERE
BY THE DEAD LINE

Sun_rising

THU LOVE IS LIKE THE
SUNRISING OF THE SUN
IT GOES DEEP DOWN IN MY HEART
IT ENCLOSED THE THOUGHT OF YOU
YOUR LOVE IN MY HEART
AND KEEP ME IN LOVE WITH YOU
THE RISING OF YOUR LOVE ON
MY MIND

NEVER'THE'LESS

MY BELOVE
I WILL ALWAYS
LOVE YOU DISTANCE
WILL NOT TAKE AWAY
MY LOVE FOR YOU
I WILL LOVE YOU IN THIS
LAND AND I WILL STILL
LOVE YOU IN A STRANGE
LAND FOR I AM IN LOVE WITH YOU
AND THAT FOR EVER
NEVERTHELESS I LOVE YOU
AND WILL AL_WAY
_____ FARE_WELL MY BELOVE

Awake

WORDS OF LOVE AWAKE YOU IN BED
ONE NEED TO PRAY TO KEEP THEIR
SOUL ALIVE GOD IN MARRIAGE
THERE IS WORDS ALSO TO
KEEP THEIR LOVE ALIVE IN MARRIAGE
DOES THY NOT KNOW _THAT THE POET
HAS SPOKEN

GREEN_ISH

GREEN GREENISH ALL GREEN
I AM GOING TO LEAVE THIS SEEN
ALL TO GREEN
FOR THEY ALL LACK THE COURAGE TO STAND UP
FOR THE DEFENSE OF THE ___ WORD OF GOD
ALL LONG STANDING GREEN_ GREENISH

String Of Pearls

I RECEIVED PEARLS FROM THE DEPTH OF THE OCEAN
FROM MY LOVE
A GIFT TO SHOW HIS LOVE FOR ME
A STRING OF PEARLS FROM THE BOTTOM OF THE OCEAN
HE PLACED THEM AROUND MY NECK AND DID
SAY PERFECT FOR YOU
THE LADY I LOVE
A STRING OF PEARLS
ONLY FOR YOU

E_ter_nal Destruction

HELL AND DESTRUCTION ARE BEFORE US
EVERY DAY
ONE CAN AVOID
ETERNAL DESTRUCTION
BY BELIEVING AND
PRAYING AND PREACH_ING
AND REJOICING IN GOD
BY AVOID_ING HELL AND DESTRUCTION
WHILE WE LIVE
THAT WE MIGHTEST LIVE ETERNAL

MIGHTY GOD

LORD OF HOST
MIGHT GOD
JEHOVAH GOD
POWER TO LOVE
ALL POWER NO POWER
ABOVE HIM OR BELOW HIM
GREAT IN STRENGHT
PERFECT IN WORDS
CARING GOD
THAT LOVE THE WORLD
AND SAVE SOULS
MIGHT GOD THE SAVIOUR OF MY SOUL

Ladie's Fashion Show

SOME OF THE FASHION ARE RED
AND BEAUTIFUL
STILL OTHER RED AND SMART LOOKING
SOME HOT AND PINK
OTHER BLUE AND PRETTY TO
BUT WHITE ARE THE ONLY ONE THAT MATTER
THEY ARE ALL JUST FOR YOU
NO NEED TO GO SHOPPING
I HAVE ALREADY BOUGHT THEM
ALL FOR YOU

SOMETHING NEW

WHILE I SIT HERE AND ABSORB
THE SUNSHINE AND YOUR LOVE TO
DARLING ON THIS LOVELY DAY
I AM MAKING SOMETHING NEW FOR YOU
TO KEEP YOU WARM WHEN I AM AWAY

WELKIN
SKYWARD BLUE

WHEN THE WELKIN
IS BLUE AND EVERY SOUND
THAT I HEAR I THINK OF YOU
THE FRAGRANT IN YOUR VOICE
IS THE TONE OF LOVE
WHAT CAN I DO BUT LOVE YOU TO
AND ACCEPT YOUR WEDDING BAND AND LOVE TO
                    BE
THEREFORE WE WILL TOGETHER

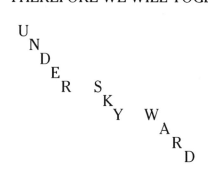

????
?
?
?

I GOT NO TIME TO DANCE OR PLAY GAMES
I AM A MARRIED MAN
I HAVE LOVED AND LOST
AND BEING REWARD AGAIN WITH LOVE
I AM A MAN NOT SEEKING FAME OR PLAYING
A LOVING GAME
FOR I GOT LOVE
AND SHE IS MY FAME
AND FAMOUS IS HER LOVE
AND WE ARE AS ONE

UNFOR_GET_TABLE

AND UNFORGETTABLE NIGHT
THAT I WILL ALWAYS REMEMBER
YOU HOLDING MY HAND IN THE CANDLE AND SINGING
I WILL BE LOVING YOU SOON
WILL YOU BE MY WIFE I WILL PAY THE
PRICE OF BEING THE FATHER AND OF
KEEPING YOU HOME
WILL YOU WEAR THIS RING AROUND YOUR NECK
UNTIL WE DO WED
THEN WE KNOW OUR LOVE IS FROM GOD ABOVE
AND UNFORGETTABLE

N
I
G
H
T

WALK_ing In The Moon_light

WALKING IN THE MOONLIGHT
TRANSPIRE LOVE IN THE NIGHT
IN THE EARLY HOURS OF THE NIGHT
STROLLING IN THE MOONLIGHT
AFTER DARK ON A SUMMER NIGHT
ONE RECEIVE LOVE AND THE
JOY OF LOVING AS YOU LIVE
THE GOING DOWN OF THE MOON
IN THE LATE HOURS OF NIGHT
BEFORE DAYS DAWN
THE BEAUTY OF THE HOLY GLOW
ONE CAN BEHOLD
AND THE JOY THAT ONE CAN BEHOLD
OBSERVING THE MOON AS IT GOES DOWN AT THE
DAWN OF DAY
WALKING IN THE MOONLIGHT TRANSPIRE LOVE
AND SO DO OBSERVING THE GOING DOWN _ INSPIRE
LOVE

UNTHINK_ABLE

MARRIAGE IS UN_THINK_ABLE
WHEN YOU PASS THE AGE LINE
OF YOUR MIND SO IS LOOSING WEIGHT
WASTE OF TIME
TO GO OUT TO DINE
WHEN YOU ARE TRYING TO
LOOSE WEIGHT
ACCEPT NO DINNER DATE
        THEN
YOU WILL BE AL_WAYS FREE
TO THINK THE UNTHINKABLE
LOOSE WEIGHT

SUNG_POEM

I WILL BE LOVING YOU SOON
I WILL BE LOVING YOU SOON
I WILL BE LOVING YOU SOON
DARLING I WILL BE LOVING YOU SOON
ALL AROUND THE ROOM
I WILL BE LOVING YOU SOON
IN THE LIGHT OF THE MOON
DARLING I WILL BE HOLDING YOU CLOSE
EMBRACED IN MY LOVE
IN THE LIGHT OF THE MOON
I WILL BE LOVING YOU SOON
IN MY ARMS
I WILL BE LOVING YOU SOON
IN THE ROOM I WILL BE LOVING YOU
SOON

HOE_DOWN

I INVITED SOME FRIENDS TO A HOEDOWN
THEY ALL CAME DRESSED IN THEIR EVEN_GOWN AND MEN WELL
DRESSED TO
I WAS DOWN IN THE COTTONFIELD
WITH INTEREST IN DURING A NIGHTS WORK
WITH MY HOEDOWN LATE IN THE
EVENING
WAITING FOR THEM TO ARRIVE
BUT THEY LOOKED UPON THE FIELD
THEN TURN BACK AND WENT TO TOWN
TO DANCE
SO I ALONE WAS PRESENT HOE_DOWN ALONE
HOEING IN THE COTTON FIELD

MY HEART

YOUR LOVE IS DRIVING ME ON
WE CAN'T BE SEPARATED
I CAN'T BARE THE FORCE OF THE ONWARD PUSH
THE URGE TO BE WITH YOU IS MUCH TO STRONG
IT BURDEN ME DOWN, FORCED JOY TO FLEE MY SOUL
IT GOT ME CLIMBING THE SKY, HIGH IN THE AIR
SITTING ON THE WALL OF THE SEA
SINGING LOVE SONGS ABOUT YOU
CALLING OUT YOUR NAME IN THE DEPTH OF MY HEART
AND SITTING IN THE DARK CALLING OUT TO YOU BUT
YOU ARE NOT THERE
LOOKING FOR YOU IN MY HEART
BUT YOU ARE THERE
FOR THE URGE IS MUCH TO STRONG
TO BE SEPARATED
I KNOW WHERE YOU BE_LONG
      IN MY HEART

DIVINE LOVE

I THANK GOD FOR THE FLAVOR
OF DIVINE LOVE
AND THE SUBSTANCE THAT IT GIVES IS
JOY
AND THE WAY IT MAKE ME FEEL IS HOLY
AND THE PRAISE
I CAN SING TO GLORIFY HIS NAME
AND I CAN LIVE FAWLESS EVERY_DAY
THAT I TRY, AND BE WISE
FOR I GOT GOD IN MY HEART AND
HE IS THAT DIVINE LOVE

CALL ME

IF YOU ARE
LONESOME AND DONT WANT TO BE ALONE
CALL ME
I WILL COME
LIKE THE FLYING WIND
THAT DONT BEND
IF YOU CALL ME
I WILL COME LIKE
A FLASH OF LIGHT IN THE DARK NIGHT
IF YOU CALL ME I WILL COME AND LIGHT
UP YOUR LIFE
IF YOU CALL ME_
I WILL AND SING YOU A SONG

TRUE SAYING

IF YOU ARE PLACE ON
STAND BY LOVE
LET THE MAN WALK ON
AND STAND BY HIM
LIFT UP YOUR HANDS TO GOD
AND PRAISE HIM AND STAND BY HIM
A TRUE SAYING FOR MORTAL MAN

DARKNESS

I STARTED TO WRITE A POEM
IN HONOR OF SOME FORMER FRIENDS
BUT I CONSIDER THAT THEY ARE NO LONGER MY FRIENDS
AND MIGHT BE OFFENDED IN THE END
      PEN
SO_ I LAID MY FOUNTAIN A_SIDE
A CLOSED MY EYES
AND MY POEM WALK AWAY INTO
THE BLACK DARKNESS OF THE NIGHT
A FLEW AWAY IN THE WIND
IN THE NIGHT IN THE WIND
IN THE BLACK, DARKNESS OF THE NIGHT

PLAYING IN THE DARK

PLAYING IN THE DARK
THE SAME OLD TUNE
TRYING TO GETOVER YOU

PLAYING IN THE DARK A NEW TUNE
ON MY STRING INSTRUMENT
TRYING TO GET NEXT TO YOU

PLAYING IN THE DARK
THE SAME OLD TUNE
TRY_ING TO KEEP YOU
PLAY_ING IN THE DARK THAT
SOON YOU WILL COME AND PLAY
THE SAME TUNE
WITH ME
PLAYING IN THE DARK
TRYING TO GET NEXT TO YOU

```
                                  A
   P   Y   N        TE  D  R
     L   _I  G  IN H      K
      A
```

SATAN AND SIN

I AM ON MY WAY TO THE
BATTLE FIELD OF MY LORD
I GOT THIS WAR TO FIGHT AGAINST
SATAN AND SIN
AND I AM FIGHTING TO WIN
AND I AM FIGHTING TO WIN IN THE END
THIS WAR AGAINST SATAN AND SIN
AND I AM FIGHTNG IN JESUS NAME
I GOT MY SWORD AND SHIELD IN MY HANDS
AND I AM FIGHTING TO WIN
THIS BATTLE AGAINST SATAN AND SIN

Marriage

WHEN I THINK ABOUT YOU

I THINK ABOUT HAPPINESS

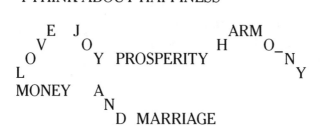

```
        E   J                         ARM
      V       O                     H      O
    O           Y   PROSPERITY             N
  L                                          Y
  MONEY      A
              N
                D   MARRIAGE
```

AND THE CHILDREN WE WILL BEAR

AND HOW WE WILL KNELL AND PRAY TOGETHER

AND THE GRIEF WE MIGHT SHARE

AND SONGS WE WILL SING TOGHTER

AND NEVER DEPART

                        SO I SAY YES

                        I WILL MARRIAGE YOU
                        _____ MARRY YOU ____

DI_PLO_MA

FOR I WILL ALWAYS REMEMBER
THAT MAYDAY THAT MYSON
RECEIVED HIS DIPLOMA
HE EXIT THE SCHOOL DOOR
DIDN'T TURN AROUND AND RAN
TO TOWN AND SOLD HIS GOWN
      LUG_GAGE
BOUGHT A BAG AND PACKED HIS
RAGS AND LEFT TOWN

DITTY DITTIES

10 DITTIES DID I HEAR IN THE WINDY
WIND
SINGING SONG OF LOVE ABOUT YOU
I HELD OUT MY ARMS AND THEY ALL
CAME TO ME_____
10 DITTIES AND NONE WAS LEFT BE_HIND

i received them in the windy wind
10 DITTIES DID I HEAR SING_ING IN THE
WIND

in
MY HEART

THE SKY IS BLUE AND SO AM _I

i FEEL SAD AND BLUE

BE_CAUSE I CAN'T bE NEAR yOU

I TURN AND GROAN and MOAN IN mY

SLEEP ^{A}N$_D$ REA^C^{H} OUT FOR yOU

I CAN FEEL YOUR LOVE IT CLOSE TO mE

FOr I LOVE YOUR VOICe IT STIMULATE ME

YOUR FACIAL EXPRESSION EX_CITE ME
YOU SPEAK WITH AUTHORITY TO CONTROL

AND I WOULD LOVE TO BE THAT ONE FOR YOU TO

CONTROL IN YOUR ARMS

YOUR EXPRESSION MAKE ME YARN FOR YOU
IT GREIVE MY HEART BECAUSE I CAN'T BE NEAR YOU

AND I WILL WALK AWAY WITH TEARS IN MY EYES

AND PAIN IN MY HEART

AND DENY THE THOUGHTS OF   Y
        O
          U

ANCIENT IN AGE

I AM ANCIENT IN AGE
STRICT IN TIME
BOLD IN WORDS
COURAGE IN WISDOM
WISE IN LOVE
STRUGGLE AND STUMBLE FAR
BUT NOT THAT FAR
THAT IT WAS TO FAR TO GET HERE
NOW THAT I AM HERE
I WILL CONTINUE TO MOVE ON
FAR FROM HERE

MOURNFUL

WHEN GOER GO BEFORE GOD
AND LEAVE THERE THEIR PRAYER IN A FOOT_PRINT
OF MOANING
WHEN ONE START MOANING TO GOD TO EXPRESS
THEIR GREIF OF SORROW
GOD HEAR THEIR SORROW
BEAR THEIR BURDEN
GIVE ONE HOPE THEIR FOOT_ PRINT
OF PRAYER WERE RECEIVED
AND JOY CLOUDS AWAY SORROW
FOR FAITH FULFIL TOMORROW
SORROW WILL CEASE WHEN GOER GO BEFORE
GOD IN PRAYER

SOUND EF_FECT

THE MELODY OF THE SOUND
SOUNDED LIKE HOLY ANGLES SINGING
FROM A DISTANCE
I COULD BEARLY
HEAR THE VOICE OF THE SOUND
BUT I KNEW IT WAS FROM GOD
FOR HOLINESS
WAS IN THE SOUND IT TOUCH MY HEART
AND I START TO CRYING
ROLL OUT OF BED AND SAID
I AM GOING TO THE HOUSE OF GOD
IN PRAYER IN MY HEART THE
SOUND MOVE ME

DECEPTION

GOD IS TRUE
THERE IS NO DECEPTION
ILLUSION OR ERROR IN HIS LOVE
UNDENIABLE PURE
FREE FROM DECEPTION
PLAINLY TRUE
HIGHLY NEEDED
SOME MEN CHERISH
OTHERS REJECT IT
CERTAINLY WITHOUT HARM OR DOUBT
RECORDED AND KNOWN TO ALL
THAT WILL HEAR HIS WORD
AND RECEIVE HIS SPIRIT
NO DECEPTION ALLOWED

BIAS--------

be not bias and mingle thy
in fault
in dealing with others
god will reward
you accord-ing to your bias
doing
be not thy bias

ZONE

IN GOD HOUSE
THERE IS NO ZONES
ACCORDING TO HIS WORD
BUT THE GIFTS OF GOD IS ENCIRCLE
RERESERVED FOR DIFFERENT PURPOSE
THEY ARE GIVEN BY ZONE FOR THE
PURPOSE GIVEN
AND REQUIRED TO BE PERSERVED
AND RESERVED BY ZONE
BY HIS SERVANTS

WAY'S OF THE WORLD

LET NOT THE WORDS OF THE WORLD
NOR THE WAYS OF THE WORLD LURE YOU
AWAY FROM CHRIST
FOR HE GAVE HIS SON LIFE
FOR ALL MANKIND
BECAUSE OF HIS LOVE
BECAUSE OF HIS LOVE HE GAVE HIS SON
LIFE FOR ALL
FOR HE SHEED HIS BLOOD ON THAT CROSS
FOR THE WORLD

LANDMARK
A GUIDE

LET GOD WORD BE A LAND-MARK FOR ALL NATIONS
LET GOD WORD BE OUR GUIDE
TO LEAD US OUT OF DARKNESS
LET US NOT WITHDRAW OUR VOICE
FROM PRAYING TO GOD
LET GOD WORD SHOW US THE WAY
IN GOD AND NOT MAN LET US CEASE
NOT TO PRAY
LET US BE FOLLOWER ALL THE WAY
OF THAT LANDMARK OUR GUIDE
THAT WILL NEVER FADE AWAY
CHRIST THE SAVIOR OF THE WORLD

BORN_AGAIN

WHEN ONE TAKE A STAND
AND HOLD OUT AND BECOME HOGGISH
HOGGED THEIR HOLD ON SIN
AND REFUSE TO GIVE IN
AND CONTINUE TO HOLD THEIR HOLD
FOR THE WAR THAT THEY WANT WIN
WHEN GOD COME IN
HE WILL MAKE WAR TO CEASE
AND DESTROY THEIR SINS
AND CAST THEM DOWN AND BOUND IN CHAIN
UNTIL THEY GIVE IN
GIVE THEM LOVE
UNTIL THEY CRY
LORD I WANT TO BE
BORN AGAIN

PLAN ATTACK WITH A POEM

I AM NOT GOING TO ATTACK YOU WITH A BOMB
BUT WITH A POEM
I WILL NOT BE DISCOURAGED BY YOUR WORDS
I AM GOING TO TELL YOU WHAT I HAVE HEARED
AND TELL IT IN A POEM

STRUCT_TING

WHEN BLUESTOCKING COME TO TOWN
PAY NO ATTENTION TO THE MEN WHEN
THEY START STRUTTING AROUND
THEY ARE ONLY LOOKING FOR THE
OPPORTUNITY TO EN_RICH THEIR LIVES
TO BE BRILLANT
BY KNOWING WHAT HOLDS YOUR INTEREST
STAND NOT IN THE LINE NEAR THEM
PAY NO ATTENTION TO THEM
AND THEY WILL STOP STRUTTING AROUND YOU

COVERED

THE WORLD IS NOT COVERED
THE WORLD IS BOLD AND WHOLE
MUCH WISDOM AND KNOWLEDGE
MANY BOOKS AND MONEY
TO SAVE AND HOLD
BUT THE WORLD IS NOT COVERED
BY THE BLOOD
THE BLOOD OF JESUS

DINE

LET GO OUT TO DINE
SOMEWHERE THAT THE PLACE IS
NICE AND FINE
SO OTHER CAN SEE WHO I AM
WHILE WE DINE AND EAT
AND I AUTOGRAPH THOSE
BOOKS OF MINES FOR MY FANS
WHILE WE DINE

FOUND A LOVE

I FOUND A LOVE
THAT WILL LAST
HE CLEAN ME WITH HIS BLOOD
AND FILL ME WITH HIS LOVE
FOR I GOT A LOVE
I FOUND A LOVE THAT WILL LAST
I FOUND THE LORD JESUS CHRIST

SOME_TIME

SOMETIME LOVE CAN CAUSE YOU TO
FLY IN THE WATER
CRAWL ON THE FLOOR
WRITE IN THE DARK
ROAM THROUGH THE HOUSE
READ WITH YOUR EYES CLOSED
EAT WITHOUT FOOD
AND LIVE A LIE AND
SMILE WHEN YOU ARE HURTING IN
YOUR HEART
SOMETIME

FOUNTAINPEN

I HAD A BALL ALL LAST NIGHT
LOOKING AT THE WALLS AND TALKING
TO THE FOUNTAIN PEN
YOU OUGHT TO SEE THE THINS IT WROTE
LAST NIGHT
MY PEN DIDN'T MISS A WORD
BUT IT WROTE IT ALL LAST NIGHT

SATAN TRYED TO ENTER TO PLAY THE
BASELINE BUT HE WAS KICKED OF THE
FIELD AND STRAIGHT TO HELL AND
CAN NOT RETURN THERE HE SHALL BE BOUND
I HAD A BALL TALKING TO THE FOUNTAIN
PEN

DON AND MARY

WRIT SOMETHING NICE ABOUT US

DON AND MARY

WRITE SOMETHING NICE ABOUT ME
AND YOU TO WE WERE IN LOVE
BUT OUR LOVE DIDN'T LAST
WE ARE STILL FRIEND BUT NO OUR
DISTANCE
        AND SMILE WHEN WE PASS ON THE
           STREET

      MARY AND DON

Printed in the United States
By Bookmasters